Germs Are Everywhere

by Rod Barkman

Minneapolis, Minnesota

Credits
All images are courtesy of Shutterstock.com, unless otherwise specified. With thanks to Getty Images, Thinkstock Photo, Adobe Stock, and iStockphoto.
Cover – Svetlana Shamshurina. Recurring – ONYXprj, robuart, Anatolir. 4–5 – ONYXprj, Abdelrahman_Mahrous. 6–7 – OlgaReukova, Billion Photos, William. 8–9 – Valentina Lev, Bernardo Emanuelle. 10–11 – hvostik. 12–13 – Andrey Sedoy, ONYXprj, Creativika Graphics, Dzm1try, Colorcocktail, CuteCute, eggeegg, Bowonpat Sakaew, nelea33. 14–15 – Tartila, Naddya, Prostock-studio, Maglara. 16–17 – Alter-ego, alazur. ClassicVector. 20–21 – Yuganov Konstantin, yusufdemirci, Yuliia Konakhovska, ElsvanderGun. 22–23 – Ailisa, mything, Spreadthesign, mexrix.

Library of Congress Cataloging-in-Publication Data

Names: Barkman, Rod, author.
Title: Germs are everywhere / by Rod Barkman.
Description: Fusion books. | Minneapolis, Minnesota : Bearport Publishing Company, [2025] | Series: Too small to see | Includes index.
Identifiers: LCCN 2023059661 (print) | LCCN 2023059662 (ebook) | ISBN 9798889169703 (library binding) | ISBN 9798892324922 (paperback) | ISBN 9798892321327 (ebook)
Subjects: LCSH: Microbiology--Juvenile literature. | Bacteria--Juvenile literature. | Viruses--Juvenile literature. | Microorganisms--Juvenile literature.
Classification: LCC QR57 .B375 2025 (print) | LCC QR57 (ebook) | DDC 579--dc23/eng/20240118
LC record available at https://lccn.loc.gov/2023059661
LC ebook record available at https://lccn.loc.gov/2023059662

Bearport Publishing is a division of Chrysalis Education Group.

For more information, write to Bearport Publishing, 5357 Penn Avenue South, Minneapolis, MN 55419.

Contents

Too Small to See

Look around the room. What is the smallest thing you can see? Try to imagine something even smaller.

Germs are so itty-bitty that we can't spot them with our eyes alone. They are all around us all the time!

Meet the Germs

Let's meet three main types of germs.

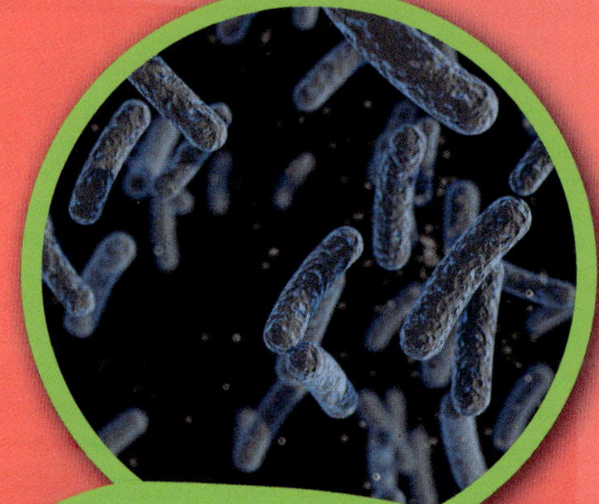

Nice to meet you. I'm a **bacterium** (bak-TEER-ee-uhm). Most of my bacteria friends are good, but some cause problems!

Hey there!
I'm a **virus**. Sorry, but viruses and humans don't always get along.
Hi, I'm a **fungus**. Some of my fungi friends are nice. Others are troublemakers.

You Make Me Sick!

Most germs around us are safe, but some can be bad for us. If those germs get into our bodies they can make us feel sick.

Germs can make you sneeze or have a runny nose. Some may even make your **stomach** upset.

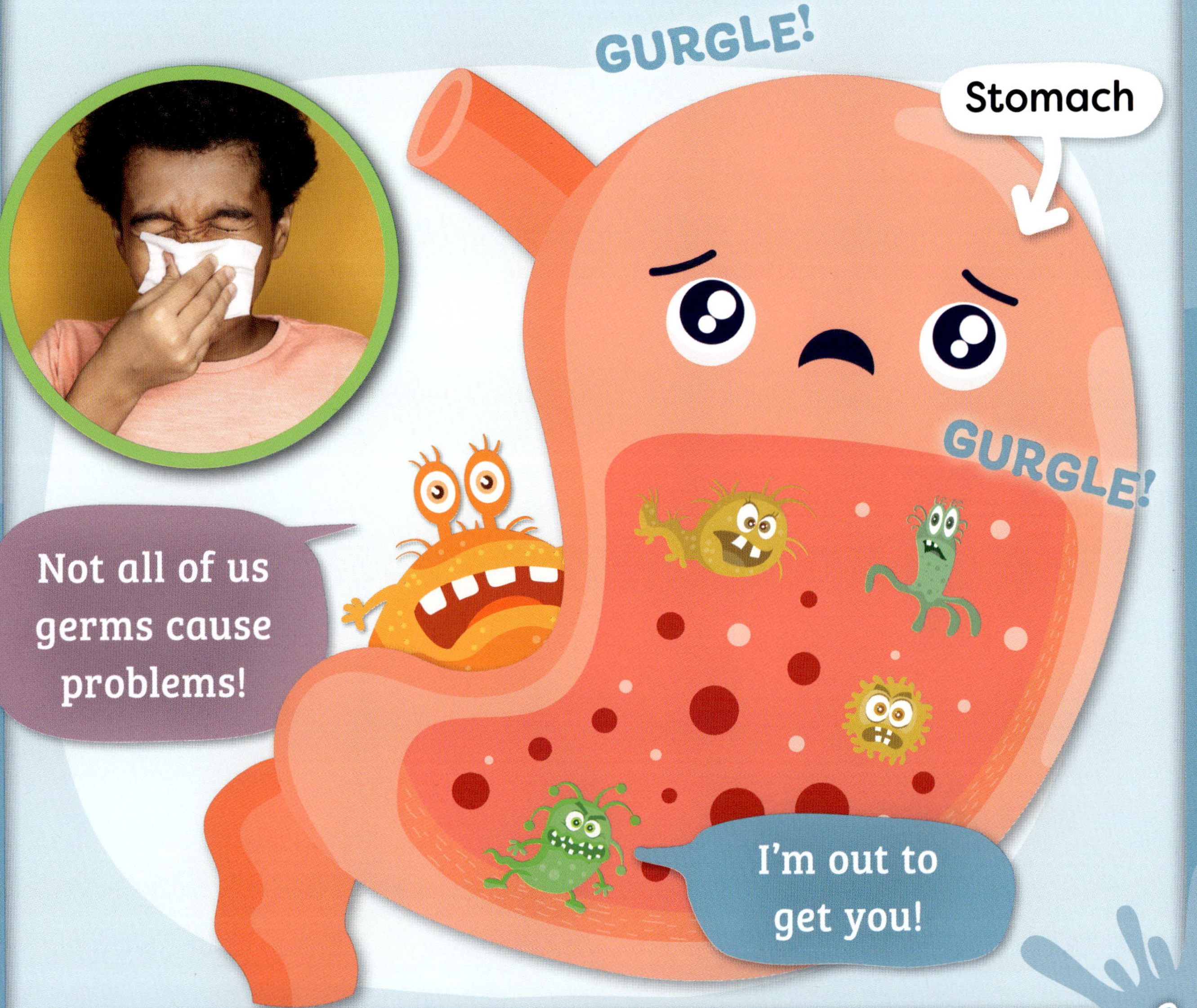

Getting Around

Germs are everywhere. They **spread** in many different ways. How can they move?

- Through the air
- In water
- On **surfaces**
- From one person's hand to another's

Wheeee!

Sure! You humans shoot me and my friends out of your noses all the time. I can also ride around in water or blow from place to place in the wind.

At Home

There are germs around us at home. Where can we find them?

Light Switches

Anywhere you touch often gets germs! Germs can move from your hand to a switch after turning on the light.

TV Remotes

When you change channels, germs can get on a TV remote.

Dirty Silverware

Germs may get onto forks or spoons when you eat with them.

Uncooked Foods

Raw meat has germs on it. Cooking food often makes it safer to eat.

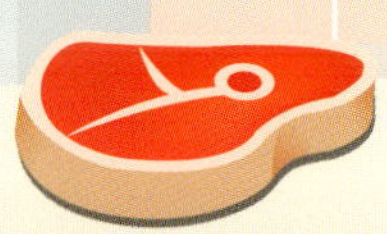

At School

Where can you find germs at school?

On your Desk

Germs can get onto desks or tables when people touch them, cough on them, or sneeze on them.

In the Air

Germs are put into the air when people breathe. A classroom with many people may have more germs.

On Pencils

When we share supplies, such as pencils, germs can be easily passed around.

Playing Sports

Sports Equipment

Lots of people in a gym share **equipment**. Things such as balls and mats are touched a lot.

Heavy Breathing

Doing sports can make you breathe hard. This means that germs can get into the air.

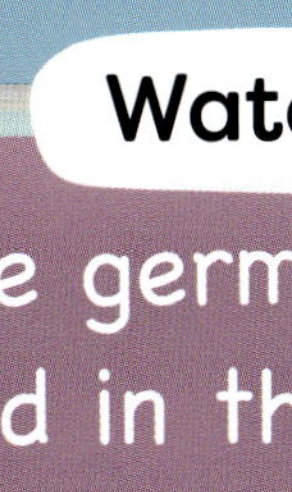

Water

Some germs can be found in the water of swimming pools.

Handrails

When you get into and out of the water, germs can pass from your hands to the handrails.

Our Bodies

There are many kinds of germs on our bodies all the time. You can't see them or feel them. Most can't harm you, but sometimes bad germs get inside.

When bad germs are in our bodies, we have help. Our **immune systems** fight germs that can make us sick. If we need extra help, a doctor can give us medicine, too.

Stop the Spread

We can also stop germs from spreading with some simple tricks!

Wash Your Hands

Wash your hands in warm water using lots of soap. Rubbing well helps get rid of most germs.

Wear a Mask

If you're sick, wear a mask. It can help stop germs from getting into the air when you breathe.

Grab a Tissue

Do you feel a sneeze coming? Grab a tissue to cover your mouth and nose! This helps stop germs from spreading.

The Good News

Many germs around us can be helpful! Here are two foods that have them.

Bread

Yeast is a type of fungus used to make bread. It lets out a gas to help bread rise. Yeast adds flavor, too.

Yogurt has lots of friendly bacteria. These germs help us break down the foods we eat. They also help stop bad germs.

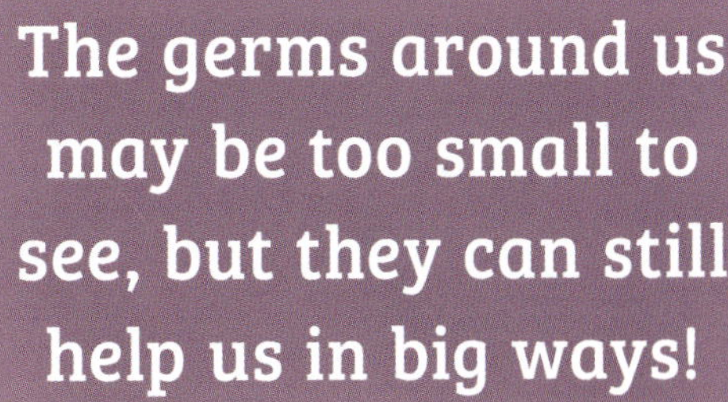

Glossary

bacterium a tiny living thing that can make you sick or keep you healthy

equipment the things used when playing sports

fungus a plantlike living thing that can't make its own food

harmless not able to hurt

immune systems the systems that bodies use to protect themselves from harmful germs

spread to move over and cover a bigger distance or area

stomach a part of the body that breaks down the food you eat

surfaces outside parts or layers of things, such as the tops of tables

virus a tiny germ that can make our bodies sick

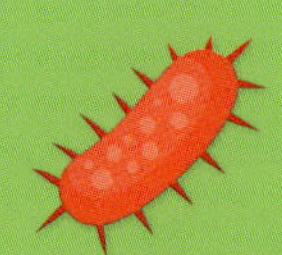

Index